LUXURY, BLUE LACE

LUXURY, BLUE LACE

S. BROOK CORFMAN
Winner of the 2018 Rising Writer Prize

 AUTUMN
HOUSE PRESS

Autumn House Press receives state arts funding support through a grant from the Pennsylvania Council on the Arts, a state agency funded by the Commonwealth of Pennsylvania, and the National Endowment for the Arts, a federal agency.

Cover art: Sarah Walko
Book & cover design: Joel W. Coggins

ISBN: 978-1-938769-36-8
Library of Congress Control Number: 2018945973

I am saying that things happened that have not been reported, and it is in virtue of those missing things that I was here. Had I spoken of them, at this point in the story, I would be elsewhere.

—Renee Gladman

Contents

I

3

PROCESSIONAL | *eight dolls*

5

LUXURY, BLUE LACE

17

PROCESSIONAL | *ten voices*

53

I

65

Notes

67

Acknowledgments

69

LUXURY, BLUE LACE

The night air bottle green and haunted and you slept, a bice pall, a presence in your room with you you felt, as you slept, following from long ago, weight at the back of your heavy head, in the middle of great fear—would you go to the lake? Would it be calming? Would you go to the forest. Dig a pit to fill and undo itself when it rains. Once upon a time, winter—no—once upon a time, a woman rose out of the ocean—no, wait—once when I was little I screamed as my father

massaged the pains from my legs. No. Tarp covering an opened home, back leaking into the cold. Here's the someone seen in a child, but whom. Terror in a house too small for fear, when your mind has the world to wield to toy with you. Knocking that stops, knocking that persists—it's not so different from the thin bed, closed door. Only barrier a blanket. If you curl so small the shape around you, breathing—he might go away, but to where—

PROCESSIONAL
(eight dolls)

2.

From the back of the drought
they arrive. Each doll, each opened eye

from within which I looked up
at myself. They fall in lines, but not the lines

I remember. Thick-knit blanket
at the fore, worn boot. She swings

from the saddle, stops at the river
to drink. Dark head of hair Grandmother

will brush, will come over and ask to do so.
How she stills.

Child always corrects
the pronunciation of her name,

saved for her a year
and defers to her, thinks of her

each moment he holds her up. Every inch
a model. Even the parted lip.

7.

She sleeps each day done, porcelain
vase, ribboned, carried forth

in her bed. Upright she wakes, closes

when she falls down.
Only hard slats, no mattress, delicate design: dust like vines

matching at first the pattern
of the headboard

before exceeding it.

3.

      Off the path a favorite
finds a field, green wild grass and small

yellow wildflowers, red-haired,
      a drawing changed

as she came alive, first delivered

      in pieces, fabric, cotton puffs, yarn.
Grandmother spun

a figure, could be anyone's, made a dress,

became a quiet mouth. She keeps

losing her wig in the tussle, a face
      all asymmetry, blank with little

pops of thread. She sits for a portrait

and a portrait bears no likeness,
      a passing face mistakes her.

Child wants a look-alike,
not a brother, to be as he might one day

become. There is a circumscribed timeline
and its unfulfilled extension. She is hard-limbed,

soft-centered and sparkling
always in a skirt bought for a New Year's party,
long after the year is up.

The boxes are full
of what Child wants to wear, what he buys
for her to fold and put away.

Above her sits the tallest form, cast
from a photo, watching,
reliable from a corner.

An image returned turned round
cheeks and an ugly maroon
sweater. She is too close. She is all

proximity. She is and is
not a possibility.

[. . .].

      Sometimes a glimpse
of a thirty-eight inch form, crowned. A crinoline. How life-sized

becomes a question, whether such a form could fit
      behind a door rarely slid away.

A dream—*nothing is impossible.*

      Child would not have looked
like her anyway. Mother says,

      wanted her desperately.

4.

And then Rose, flower-named, lost
in a fantasy. She rides a horse, masquerades, boards a ship

through a mirror. Child will travel
in time, but it will be less

glamorous. Result
of sore legs, mask

rescued from a caved room.
Rose brings a key to the attic and locks it.
Downstairs she says nothing.

Or she says, it is nothing.

8.

At the end of the line, a blue mermaid
all her own. She beaches late, stranded

as the tide pulls out, and out,
            and out, and out. Small shells tremble

            beside the transparent globe, the gold-
backed hand mirror. Clasp closed and shy.
            The only token to have touched
a doll and been displayed.

1.

       If I tell you the story
I'll ruin it; I don't remember it
       to tell it, if it's a story. You can learn at least this much

without a proper sequence:
       a child, desperation, a twin brother, how the child
chooses a form but only after

is told what the options were. Tulle and taffeta rust,
       left alone. What does it take

to know yourself? A narrative? A losing

       of some things so that others

might be legible? It takes. Think of a room

       you can move around in,
to which you might one day
       return. A smaller room

in the wall, at this child's eye level,
       in which to hide.

Here's the first doll.

       Teddy bear and his shred
of faded blanket.

There's no story here

a voice says, you
        or the child or the toy
or some sound,

only movement. Only you moving.
        Only moving away.

LUXURY, BLUE LACE

I.

(EXHORTATION)

In a story my mother tells, my name is David and it is not my fault. In another, another name, and another child, and there is no more ambiguity to such a title. A glint at the corner of your eye, that pulls you toward the window. A series of stained glass. I am the little miss cursed to drip gems from her lips, the boy whose midnight speaks locusts and dragonflies. They flee from me, these only friends. In this story I've already ended, in this story I'm everybody's love. Each plague to name. Each undoing. Please stay with me while I try. I am not sure how to explain.

(WEIGHT)

Rip in the sky. Red light dusting my impression in the dirt.

I was following that red contour, marked trail. An excess of borders ridging up
the topsoil.

Walking breaks into broken ground. It feels different where a path's been laid.

Pound of rust or package of gossamer. Equal volumes sink to different depths.

We measure displaced earth to assign value to a particular body, unable to look
directly at it.

I began filling the outline, the dirt reflective, and breached the border.

To measure one value, we choose imprecision in the measure of another.

An aggregation of ashes or a disturbance in sand.

(THE CRISIS)

I can feel myself saying, I used to want to be a girl—

long years of brackets close again in lines.
Fault from rock split space into which a sad animal,
plush, was placed.

It opens. It does not end there.

Only beauty still moves me a dead man writes. The wrong path, or is it,

that in such forms I hope to find a through line, a past
no longer past. It is not that I want to be afraid, but I am.

I face my back to the door find myself
pulled forward as the exiting force.

Where will what wind carry me when I say it:

I have been lying to myself again.

Let one word go even as another does not suggest itself

(THE CRISIS II)

I tell the therapist this, that I used to want to be a girl

but can't remember what that meant, or decide

what remains. She says, are we talking about making changes

or just congruency? and suggests how I feel about my father.

I don't mean to hurt him, but it is not true.

Granite counter on which twin boys are placed.

I love my father, I

had no idea what to do with him.

Or it is true the erotic can be other than sexual. I wanted to stay small and held.

When the therapist guesses my sexual role, as if such a thing were certain,

it's not important whether she was right, I think, even though she was.

It's more important that she doesn't think of me

as a pathology, even as all I know of her

is what she tells me. She says it's not uncommon, but I gave up a thin piece of fabric

and without it, comfort has been difficult to recognize.

Little daughter,
what did you know? When you felt unnamable

pressure, drew shapes
instead of people, faces

that became blue triangles,
red squares.

Today I tried to draw those shapes again,
arbitrary circles,

and with each attempt thought, how
when I cannot even steady a line.

(MATRILINEAL)

My mother and I, in the interval between then and now, we spoke of desire only
sparingly.

Each iteration became the others until there was a curtain of delicately sewn
crystals across my face.

But when she made a new friend, a psychologist, and she told him about me. It
seemed to be time.

We have the discussion over wine, at a dinner, at a family outing to an art gallery,
at a coffee shop.

The walls of the grotto fade in and out of the walls of the home.

The psychologist says if I were a child now he would advise my parents to
proceed differently.

To help the child manifest their conviction of a certain self-knowledge.

A conviction of self I cannot recover, if I had it.

There is a difference between remembering a thought and remembering what it
felt like to have it.

The exchange of mermaids for a navy blue field. A coercion.

For safety, ease, the ease of others. Lone birch.

A cubist portrait speaks, says this is part of maturity.

But the troubled feeling is present whether or not it is expressed.

She writes poems about her own mother.

An imaginary middle between two points.

Each crumbling paper bridge carefully held.

(TELEPATHY)

There is the imaginary twin (blue) and the real twin (red), as if we can know
beforehand the distinction.

We shared a face. We both tried to hide. Each named slant for a patriarch.

Dysphoria of many kinds, but some more striking than others: long hair, closed
doors, scales, the dragging back from other rooms to the one that breathed
softly as it slept.

I covered the oak chest in my chest, dumped it in the lake, swam back and forth
over its sunk weight, endless anchored line.

I left everyone who had seen it open behind, except my family, who I couldn't.
They were polite. They never brought it up.

What is normal, everyone asks, and I repeat any answer back.

My brother moved forward, became a lawyer. I thought to dredge the chest, to
see if or where its wood had rotted.

Left it in the lake.

(The dead man again: *See, I'm already not crying. That's enough.*)

It's easy to hide as what's expected. The hard part is, later, convincing them that
you're not.

Now we're apart and have to remember to speak. We assume we have, and
recently.

Telepathy, like ease, is a lie.

And yet we're rarely surprised.

(ONE MINUTE)

Here is a difference between us
—no, wait—
here it is. Here is the only one:

that I was picked first by gloved hands.

Everything else is fingerprints,
each groove worn as a response

to a psychiatrist who told me his job
was to encourage acceptance

of meaninglessness

but the world is sticky and it sticks to me
even though I have often wanted
to be rid of it.

(CAUTION)

I am trying to talk about the deepening without talking about darkness.

The seriousness of the glacier, the way it doesn't melt but hardens in the sun.

Bring your pickaxes and your small boxes of matches.

The layers refract sight from the center better than opacity hides any blue core.

I am tired of using black and white as symbols for despair and hope, as if they are
abstractions.

Often darkness saved me.

Sometimes still I am alone.

Sometimes still I kill the sea creature headed for the surface.

Here is a dead piece of coral that never lived.

This is my mind and this is my mind in the net, chewed by the ski boat's engine.

It feels like the gaps in a series of absences.

(SCRIM)

The child is opaque,
but here is an expression

of pain, as language shifts
from description

to wish. Wish told no.
For A, the emotion

is constant, new language
a new way to ask

the same thing of her listener.
For B, do different words

come from different emotions?
The child is opaque.

B might be trying
to get what is wanted

a different way, or B might have decided
he wanted something else.

When one is on the cusp,
has a wishing well

or a first star seen
each bright night,

and the cusp wanes. The child
is opaque and soon lost

even to the child.
Even to the child

no longer a child.
But if I am still young, the fear

or the wish—
it rises to meet what scrim

of threat, that a changing form
changes not, outwardly, at all—

II.

(OBSCURE/CLEAR)

In *La Grande Jatte*, Georges Seurat restretched each dot to be within an eye's
transition. He made his own outside judgment and the colors came together.

Crowded negative space, waves wrinkled like paper, let no light filter the floor.

Did cutting once have harmony—now an age gone by, some arbitrary slips in, or
was there, or was cut but never random—

I exalt these waters. I stir this space before me.

In Pittsburgh, the James Turrell floor of the museum flanks with blue and with red
the watching of your eyes as they adjust.

Multiple circles, multiple hues.

—and rotate and rotate and rotate and rotate and—

Someone once told me I was California, all beaches and hints of forest fire.

We're made of paper; we're all overlapping. Some glue, some fit. One space
fractured of dots. Barely any brightly colored chrysanthemums.

No footing but the waters, writes Susan Howe.

The feluccas, in the morning, heading out. The feluccas, all at once, heading in.

Kid, the tell is not the way you dress but whether or not you say no.

Is it a luxury to outgrow desire, blue lace?

A filter across the door. Hammer to hands certain nails and slip through.

Clear over flesh looks painted pink. Shrink-wrap your skin away.

Remember the game in which you were chased but never caught?

Where if you stopped running you could keep the distance you'd earned?

Keep playing that one, long after the boys stop chasing you on the playground.

Oh kid, your parents are crying over what your face could do to the world.

Not your face. Some screen in front of it that communicates.

Wolf in wolf's clothing,

but the pelt, pink and trimmed with busy-patterned fabric, it twirls
with the boy—ask him—what is a red fox, years later, on the head—
someone says this is a problem—the color of liquor through
the day—wolf's clothing will not warm like natural
hide—

but the pelt a pretty he will shiver off, for a hide to stretch
and pain a side under ribs, that will not let him give
way—will keep memory of a twirl long
after it has shredded—

twice-carved caves inside—

one woman wore bubbles—another, androgyny—
and you touched each of their arms—even that spirit—

There was a bowl of clear water swum in like a lake.

There was hide. There was no.

My strangled form in the purple room, paint all over in cream and red.

The carpet will still show through.

We all go through phases. This phase is rigid until the end.

Phase of mind-over-woken. Friction, cold.

Not-lost puzzle piece, we put together the picture without you.

A little valueless showing through.

This octagon, a form known well, shattered along stress lines.

A form that falls perfectly apart.

A set of glassworker's tools.

A daily practice.

Even when you open up one box from the attic.

Fine threads of cloth frayed by the hinge.

You suspected there was another, richer wood and older.

Wilted and dried inside, but preserved.

I still walk incorrectly.

I am noticeable in a crowd
if the crowd moves. Distinguishable

from an impression.

Too much
hip for a boy less than a man. Does walking

mean walking a runway, to put oneself on show.
Sometimes I invent a more straight-

forward stride, landing not one in front of the other

but in two lines. Doesn't it hurt you to run,
to land so heavily?

It hurts to force apart a line.

Here are three signs: (1) I am (2) I hate (3) I should have been.

This is the comfortable trap, the safety of it, shorn.

That a third of the application is filled out correctly, whether or not it has been
established that a third is a significant amount. Whether or not a third
sufficiently indicates belief.

Evidence and claim, to fabricate them into being.

A girl who counts to seven to keep at bay the tides. She survives, but the rock on
which she stood is crushed.

Like her, I seem to know only that at which I have failed.

A new alignment, without changing either the beginning or the end.

I didn't want to hurt myself, the consequences
of a wish like hair falling away. Gossip
me to the base of the turret I imagined,

that holds the soft but plastic skins.
I use these custom-crafted gloves to climb
the stones, etched lines of heat between malice and mis-
take, a shore as evening turns sadness

into dancing lights, alone in my iris.
When I don't know what to say I say fraught,
walk around with threadborn, straining hearts. If I call it
a mistake I won't know who to forgive.

Someone to let go of my hand and let me—

The long ago words of my mother, gait of my father.

Earl Grey prophecy, a playground, no, not here either—

Candied jewel holding a stare fixed ahead—

In kindergarten you were married, and what kind of ring did you use, which vow?

Each whispered spill and no net in sight, pulled taut, nothing to catch—

Why stay, why move toward that fenced field? Is it an edge?

(TRACE/TEXTURE)

I, a made thing, a deep-textured skin.

Between us are fogs, hazy wind chimes through my blue cylinder surroundings. A
handprint on one side matches but not perfectly a handprint on the other.

For a long time I didn't build myself, thought I did but crafted only those shapes on
the surface. A friend says, you grew up in a year, maybe two. But only after.

I thought I needed people only as flowers.

If I'm supposed to be mature everyone else has still been practicing for much
longer; people keep saying I'm confident, but it seems my only options are
speak and vanish.

I was on that fine line between wanting.

Which danger was the more important one, pressing in: when a beautiful man
spoke to me all I could say was this panic is rising like a panic.

I started thinking about the thing I made when I thought I was making myself.

A door I kept leaving open, so that you could see the wall.

Perhaps a hybrid thing is the thing that looks like a man but was made in the ocean.

The shock of the person walking around when you realize: the person is you.

To have cried so little in sixteen years—once, twice—and to have marked each time.
To have cried for the vanishing dream in which I would never cry again.

III.

Dear docent,

        take me on the journey from not imagined to conceivable:
some rumor of delirium,
    of cities breaking you into several people at once.

We made a city, a nasty one, and now we have to live in it,
        our memory a latecomer.
  Our tiny pulses, the breath.

          Someone says, You do not form
       yet you will make a space, and
               he can mean you can mean I.
    Sometimes a lover, or a projection.

Forgive me then this my crime: that I saw you

where you were not.
    Your voice a house

    built entirely of doors.
  The eye an errant thing, a mode of forgetting.
I take no less than that,

than skies for earths
  and a ceiling paved in aquatic light.

      I exhaust our little moment.

(AN ORCHID)

I've begun meditation, but don't know what it should be helping to clear.

An ordered array of expectations, a contiguous line outwards.

Today a rainforest canopy of rooftops. Impossible brown leaf of a drowning tree.

You bloom in my mind, an orchid. A glassed-in relic.

The machine in your ear I sometimes hear instead of you.

I'm writing in blue because words are not water.

I'm practicing desire.

Free radicals unspool the atmosphere.

(ODD HOUSE)

What of a life wrapped in thread is vaunted.

An odd house, memory, certain doors toward anachronism. A decayed wall.

When I hallucinated a spider web I imagined a wedding dress, pristine and
impossible to dust.

A wrought-iron bed to lie in while holding court.

Over everything threads, threads played like a violin, the taut ones, the ones
coming down without sound.

When I lift the suitcase, I must be sick, I am so weak. But the suitcase is filled
with rocks, with books, nothing I would have thought to hide away.

Traces of memory like oil across glass, smudged from use, a hot, crowded emotion.

You once told me a chair is just not interesting enough, but I think it is, it is, when
one cannot sit in it.

What would you think of me now, sometimes still unable to leave this tight-wound
home.

Small bells and their occasional ringing, their pulls plucked.

From the tall dresser at the entrance, individual hands knot.

(DUET)

You like to ask rhetorical questions. I like timelines. I see in them only gaps, how I'm on the other side of the river from the grandfather clock in your head. Sometimes I make my own holes, chipping away at the mortar to achieve a handmade effect. My time is the slow construction of an obelisk with an agitated heartbeat. Yours whiskey and changing orbits. We make both from bricks laid out in the sun all day. This isn't labor, just dabbling. In one timeline I was alone; in another you were someone else. I stay quiet among all these throats tuning themselves. When I sing I lose my voice. Yelling with a streak of blue. Sometimes we risk it and perform an exuberant rendition of what's really a very sad song. For a time my feet were wood, dark oak, and so much cold gathered in them.

(BORROWED STONE)

A steady gaze fills a particular kind of space.

I could pinch it, so I do, seeking beneath the barrier.

The first time I pierced my ear, the winged fish fell from the sky, punctured.

My fingers dig and pierce again, again, after a hollow's itch.

Men's fingers point to what holds magic, condemn its thin contour.

Thus pricked, a collapse and burial. Wildflowers bloom above me.

The pretty girls clutching teddy bears mourn, feathered to the ground.

Felled by stones thrown from whose fingers—men's, mine.

Deadened down. Holes up the sleeve.

Even witchery cannot lift such weight.

(HERMIT AND HERMETIC)

True, an attic dweller   a turret.

Proximity is a window   a cage of careful paper

fitted tightly on a face.   *To know me as golden is to know me*

all wrong. I am afraid   of myself, or, I am unwilling

to share.   I might have chosen otherwise.

A small fist   pounds the moment

you woke in the hourglass   lilies at the hinge

of your neck. If you move to touch them   they move inside

the predictable rebuke: No more

(TRANSMUTE)

With only a skimmed finger-touch I invent a memory. A clarity of ritualized
motion.

If I had seven lives, when I was burnt, or drowned, and if I drowned in water or
molten rock—

I could have been an alchemy. Lead to lead, into something pure.

Blank space takes up weight. An ingot. Platinum is often a metal rid of earth—

Does that make it pure. Can you get a good glimpse of yourself.

Cling to the explosions in the helmet—platinum, too. You might look better that way.

I turned to the window and thought volcanoes were clouds.

A room filled with whatever such rooms are filled with. A sweat-stuck something else.

The focus moves from one thing to wilderness, a single point circling.

If you took my head, I'd know what to look at. But how could I show you my head.

(TRANSPARENCY)

Tell me what it's like to hear your insecurities in the timbre and the backstep of your voice. Charming or a tone too high. There's biology connecting one trait to another through the leaves. A network of them below my ribs, in the small chambers we don't think the voice comes from. Instead a reservoir of air. Unless I'm all in my head, this voice finds every space to ring. You need breath support and tone, but I've trained my lungs for years. My head lets some of that down. Maybe there won't be a performance, but there will be singing of a kind. I grew up in that house, humming. Even when I opened the windows, I never tried to remove the screens.

(OMEN)

A room as antechamber, to what. Fear as imminent presence, but nothing appears.

I close the blinds as a seal; I turn the light on to calm down; I imagine music; I
    replace the imaginary with the real.

Still, I cannot shake the shape each sensation takes.

When you sounded, I thought you'd been addressing me.

I kept thinking no one would notice if I vanished and remembering people who
    might.

A peach tree orchard in bloom, just as the heavy feeling arrived.

Here's the space between two people, which is the same as the space between
    three, between four, between one.

PROCESSIONAL
(ten voices)

First Revenant:

I once was a man who tried to be sad but found it difficult. I was once a woman who had more success. An everyday malaise, a balloon without the air. I would go to the French patisserie down the street and sit there, thinking, is this sadness? Then, later, thinking, is this?

Second Revenant:

Once upon a time we were twins and we were two and there were two of us. We didn't know difference except that there was one.

Once upon a time we let each other cut in lines, we rained from different clouds on the playground, we had to be separated.

We spoke our own language but don't remember it.

We say we are identical and the new faces are confused, they think we are both male, they say we only look enough alike to be brothers. At a certain point we do not bother to correct them.

Third Revenant:

Every time I try and fly away I end up here, in the bath, as if I can be clean. As if a bath were made of cups, mugs, of bowls—unique, similar, filled with water, too many to move without spilling them all across the floor.

The doctor says there are only three parts of a human form that need soap, that the water clears away other dirt. I never believe doctors. I never wrinkle, the osmosis of it all is confusing. Either water can clean the oil that makes me waterproof, and so can clean the oily parts of me, or it cannot.

Once I thought instead to run away to a circus, watched a tightrope walker walk up the taut rope's incline. She slipped down the wire no thicker than a wisp, no net and only the wand for balance, her hope that if she fell and waved it it would break her fall. I wanted her steadiness, but when she slipped I gasped, she paused, and I knew if I slipped I would gasp at myself and fall.

Fourth Revenant:

Sometimes I think about putting all of the money into a beach house, or a row of them, and we could all live there and walk into the ocean whenever we wanted. We wouldn't be underwater all the time but could watch the water instead, and go into it when we wanted to, and choose how far up our bodies we wanted it to reach. But of course, the waves. There is always the chance of an undertow. And does a chance seem better than a certainty, that you might not be swept away and dashed upon the rocks? A winding, a leap from a pebbled pier. I was one way of entering. A body of water was another.

Fifth Revenant:

When destiny and I got lunch, he reminded me that I am always choosing violets, that only my mother knows how to garden and when she goes the snow drops will be dead.

She planted a peach tree that died alongside one future, and it was beautiful without leaves, hung with metal rings.

I'm undoing the brightness, breathing through it toward shapes that become distinct. When I touch this point in the air a door opens, and I can never fall asleep while I'm looking through it.

Sixth, Seventh, and Eighth Revenants:

Do you love me, and what would you do for it? There's a calm surface to hold your breath under, if you've trained yourself to do so. When pain feels like failure, just because you've lasted this long doesn't mean you will the next time. Two stark landscapes, one the mountains over a frozen lake as clouds move rapidly, the other a field and a green hill above a pond in which a car has crashed, sinks. It's all silent and the wind blows the cobwebs away, the wind someone's breath, she swims away and this austerity is unbroken. Her eyes are open. Mountains are not sharp but rugged, messy, breaking into gravel every minute. Right now they are sleek. Cloud shadows pass, shapes that can be other than their projections. Not me, not mine.

Ninth Revenant:

You said there was a sequence but no story. Aren't I doing better? I'm making my own standards and judging them. I wasn't there in the car, it was one moment without me. As you said, progress. A slow unrolling of a carpet across dirt, a pristine blue muddying. Not an inevitable outcome. I wondered what I would remember and what I would forget, bringing the water with me everywhere even though I am always swimming away from it. It is like running from air—which, of course, would lead you to the lake.

Mother:

"I can still see myself standing in the kitchen. The subject changes. But I could not say the words. What kind of mistake. God just forgot. My heart breaking.

"Her own children do not dream every night of waking. In a different body. Wouldn't everything be all right. Serious, in crisis, to be worked out quickly. We are both crying.

"Immediately proud, asks if it is a good idea to allow. Considered shameful. I am getting ready. It is as if by choosing his toys he is choosing his life.

"No one says anything. Only I seem to be worried today.

"No, no, not even angst, I, desolate, feeling. A costume only I will know. Maybe.

"My words will give a certainty, to be fulfilled within his own body.

"Is that really possible?

"Filled with buried deep inside is once he finds is I am not of course not their child

"Filled with retreat, return I pick one up I am depressed the captive what a gift is

"I imagine I pick it is written with me I feel the sense of betrayal to find relief

"I go to a psychiatrist overlooking the carpets seeking affirmation we look for a new mistake

"I never let that pass I correct them I correct them I correct them I carefully instruct I give up

"I think more I am getting ready I try not to ask

"He has stopped wearing his skirt in the daytime."

You were trying to find the line and its cease. Had you made the decision or was it made for you? There are many rooms and you suffer most when you go between them. A tendency even in language to uninhabit. But now, we know there are rooms. We know it is the going from one to the other that takes it out of you. Blue room into blue room. If only facts would move forward—ellipses without elision, only gap. Where the skull meets the neck, feeling gathers as a grounding stone. Soak it in salt water, warm it in your hands. Let it settle your flickering form, rough outline. Return it to that suboccipital space. A center, or one of them. A knowledge. The stone's river or the river in your spine. Even the ocean is evaporating where it lies exposed.

Notes | *A shape's got no door.* —C.S. GISCOMBE

Epigraphs are from Renee Gladman's *Event Factory* and C. S. Giscombe's *Prairie Style*.

The "dead man" quotations are Chekhov: the first is Jean-Claude van Itallie's translation of *Uncle Vanya*, the second Sarah Ruhl's of *Three Sisters*. The poem beginning "Dear docent" is a cento with lines from Caroline Bergvall, Gwendolyn Brooks, Emily Dickinson, Jessica Fisher, Deborah Landau, Alice Notley, Claudia Rankine, Cole Swensen, Joshua Marie Wilkinson & Kazim Ali. (BORROWED STONE) covers Michelle Lin's poem "Stone"; (HERMIT AND HERMETIC) contains a line from Hillary Gravendyk's poem "Exuberance," itself modified from the Band of Horses song "The Funeral." The poem spoken by "Mother" manipulates language from an unpublished essay of my mother's.

Less linear borrowings occur in the poem beginning "Little girl," indebted to a drawing workshop by curator Liz Park; in (SCRIM), indebted to a conversation with sociologist Tey Meadow and her research on parents raising trans and gender-nonconforming children; and in (ODD HOUSE), which responds in part to Chiharu Shiota's *Trace of Memory* at the Mattress Factory (2013-2016).

In addition to the aforementioned voices & influences, these were also in the water with the poems:

- —Filament Theatre's 2011 production of Sarah Ruhl's play *Eurydice*
- —"Silent Voices," an episode of the television show *Vera* (2012)
- —*It Follows* (2015), a film by David Robert Mitchell
- —An untitled piece in Ana Mendieta's *Silueta* series, using sand and red pigment (1976)

—Barnett Newman's *Onement, I* (1948), as well as, later, the paintings of
 Agnes Martin
—Remedios Varo's paintings, especially *Tailleur Pour Dames* (1957) &
 Les Murés (1958)
—The mixed media works of Howardena Pindell collected in *Howardena
 Pindell: Paintings, 1974-1980*
—London Grammar's album *If You Wait* (2013), especially the song
 "Sights"
—Davide Panagia's work on sensation and narratocracy in *The Political
 Life of Sensation* (2009) & Audre Lorde's "The Uses of the Erotic:
 The Erotic as Power"
—Mei-Mei Berssenbrugge's poetry, especially *Concordance* (2006) and
 Hello, the Roses (2013)
—Elfriede Jelinek's *Her Not All Her,* trans. Damion Searls (2013)

Acknowledgments

Many thanks to the editors of the following journals and anthologies, in which poems in this manuscript first appeared, sometimes in different versions and/or with (different) titles:

DIAGRAM: (AN ORCHID) & (TRANSMUTE)

EMERGE 2016 Lambda Fellows Anthology: [The night air bottle green] & [Someone to let go]

Gigantic Sequins: [You were trying to find the line]

Hawai'i Review's "Occupying Va": [Wolf in wolf's clothing] & [There was a bowl of clear water]

HEArt Online: (THE CRISIS) & (SCRIM)

The Journal: (TELEPATHY)

Muzzle Magazine: Processional (*ten voices*)

PHANTOM: (DUET) & (TRANSPARENCY)

Pinwheel Journal: (ODD HOUSE)

Quarterly West: [*Dear docent*], (OBSCURE/CLEAR), (THE CRISIS II) & (CAUTION)

The Spectacle: Processional (*eight dolls*)

Twelfth House: [Kid, the tell], [I still walk], [I didn't want], [Here are three signs] & (EXHORTATION)

Washington Square Review: (TRACE/TEXTURE)

Beloved ancestors of poems in this book appeared in *Winter Tangerine*'s "Mythology of Childhood" feature, the anthology *[S O F T]* from MIEL Books, and in the collaboration "Crafting Words" with ceramic artist Juliette Walker at the Central Public Library in Madison, WI.

[The night air bottle green] also appeared as "Exordium," a poem-film with the Visible Poetry Project directed by Albert Tholen.

I am grateful for the support of Lambda Literary, Ashbery Home School, and the University of Pittsburgh, as well as for *Quarterly West*'s nomination of my work for the Best of the Net Anthology.

Thank you to:

Dawn Lundy Martin, for genius;
Stephanie Cawley, for bond;
Yona Harvey, for art;
Cory Holding, for presence;
Lynn Emanuel, for exuberance;
Angie Cruz, for beauty;
Thora Brylowe, for enthusiasm;
Claudia Rankine, for rigor;
Aaron Kunin, for economy;
Sarah Nokes-Malach, for kindness;
Elizabeth Rodriguez Fielder, for a solution;
Lauren Russell, for the turret;
Cameron Awkward-Rich, for a gift;
Michelle Lin, for letting me borrow a stone;
Richard Siken, for the impossible;
Christine Stroud, Alison Taverna, Joel W. Coggins, and Sarah Walko
for the real;
Kelly Andrews, Amanda Awanjo, and Moriah Purdy, for company;
Nico Amador, Chen Chen, Portia Elan, Elaina Ellis, Keelay Gipson, Wren Hanks, Taylor Johnson, and Joy Ladin, for example and activism;
Ariana Brown, Kazumi Chin, Sophia Geffen, Kim Grabowski Strayer,

Malcolm Friend, Efe Kabba, Lucia LoTempio, Jessica Lanay Moore,
Gabrielle Rajerison, Julia Ringo, Suzannah Spaar, Daniel Thompson,
Juliette Walker, and Caleb Washburn—my fellow travelers;
to those I've forgotten, for undeserving labor;
to Steffan Triplett, for unwarranted, unwavering belief;
and to my family—especially Mom, Dad, and Jack, for pride.

To Hillary Gravendyk, for gentle ghosts.